Egypt

Helen Arnold

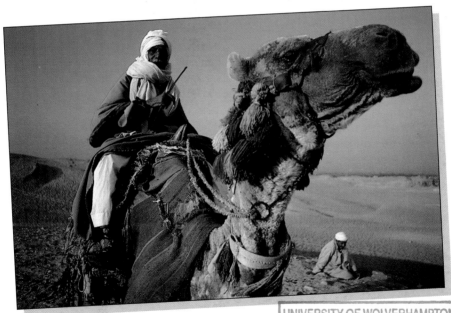

A ZOË BOOK

A ZOË BOOK

© 1996 Zoë Books Limited

Devised and produced by
Zoë Books Limited
15 Worthy Lane
Winchester
Hampshire SO23 7AB
England

First published in Great Britain in 1996 by
Zoë Books Limited
15 Worthy Lane
Winchester
Hampshire SO23 7AB

A record of the CIP data is available from the British Library.

ISBN 1 874488 75 4

Printed in Italy by Grafedit SpA
Editor: Kath Davies
Design: Sterling Associates
Map: Julian Baker
Production: Grahame Griffiths

Photographic acknowledgments

The publishers wish to acknowledge, with thanks, the following photographic sources:

Eitan Simanor - cover bl, 8; / Explorer 6; / Robert Harding Picture Library; The Hutchison Library / Jeremy A. Horner - cover r, title page, 10; / Carlos Freire 16; / Bernard Gerard 22; Neil Folberg / The Image Bank 20; Impact Photos / Ben Edwards - cover tl, 26; / Mike McQueen 12; / Colin Jones 14; / David Sillitoe 18; / Gavin Goulder 24; / Hannes Wallrafen 28.

The publishers have made every effort to trace the copyright holders, but if they have inadvertently overlooked any, they will be pleased to make the necessary arrangement at the first opportunity.

Contents

All the words that appear in **bold** are explained in the Glossary on page 30.

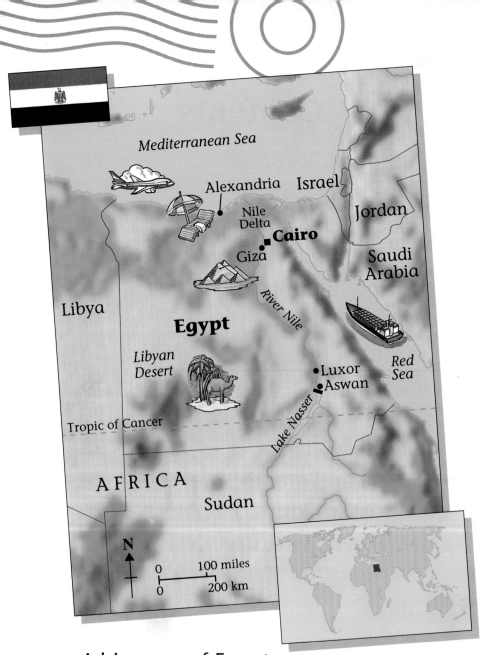

Mediterranean Sea

Alexandria   Israel

Nile
Delta   Jordan

Cairo

Giza   Saudi
Arabia

Libya

Egypt   River Nile

Libyan
Desert   Red
                       Sea
                  •Luxor
                  •Aswan

Tropic of Cancer

Lake Nasser

A F R I C A

Sudan

N

0   100 miles
0   200 km

A big map of Egypt
and a small map of the world

4

Dear Thomas,

You can see Egypt in red on the small map. It took five hours for the plane to fly here from London. Egypt is a part of Africa. The weather here is very hot and dry.

Love,

Will

P.S. Mum says that the River Nile runs through the middle of Egypt. The land next to the Nile is rich and green. This is where most of the people live.

The city of Cairo and the River Nile

Dear Mandy,

We are staying in Cairo. It is the biggest city in Africa. We went to a market called a **bazaar**. Mum bought some gold and silver jewellery.

Love,

Stephen

P.S. We cannot read the papers here! Most people in Egypt speak and write in Arabic. The letters look different from ours, and people read from the right side of the page to the left.

A fruit and vegetable market in Cairo

Dear Rod,

In Cairo we buy food from street stalls. Dad pays with Egyptian money called *piastres*. Dad likes *falaafil*. They are made of beans fried up with **spices** and shaped into little balls.

Love,

Walter

P.S. We got fresh figs and mangoes from the market. I love mangoes. They are big and sweet and juicy. Dad peels them and slices them up for us.

The Great Pyramid and the Sphinx
at Giza. The Sphinx has the head of a
person, but the body of a lion.

Dear Lucy,

The Sphinx is made of the same stone as the pyramids. They are thousands of years old. Each pyramid was built for a ruler of Egypt. The ruler was called a *pharaoh*.

Love,

Petra

P.S. Mum says that the ancient Egyptians knew how to keep, or **preserve**, dead bodies. These bodies are called mummies. When the *pharaoh* died, the mummy was put inside the pyramid.

A *felluca* on the River Nile

Dear Leroy,

We are on a big boat. It is travelling down the River Nile. Boats carry goods on the river as well. We saw a boat carrying cotton. The small sailing boats are called *fellucas*.

Your friend,

Wesley

P.S. We saw a train going along beside the Nile. Mum and I like the boats better. They are cooler than the trains and buses. The buses here are full of people.

A ferry boat takes people and animals across the Nile.

Dear George,

We are in the Nile **Delta**. This is where the River Nile joins the sea. It splits up into lots of little rivers. Sometimes the river floods. This is good for farming.

Love,

Robby

P.S. Dad likes watching the *shaduf*. It is a **machine** for watering the land. It is a bit like a see-saw. There is a bucket on one end of a pole and a weight at the other end.

Mending fishing nets in Alexandria

Dear Jean,

I really like this city. It is called Alexandria and it is beside the sea. The sea is warm. It is blue and clear. People come here for holidays. They like to swim and sit on the beach.

Love,

Thelma

P.S. Dad says that people in Alexandria work very hard. We saw lots of fishing boats and some fishermen drying their nets.

The Temple of Karnak at Luxor

Dear Laurie,

This one of the oldest places I have ever seen. It is called Luxor. Kings and queens who ruled Egypt are buried here. They lived thousands of years ago. People come here to visit the **temples**.

Love

Henry

P.S. Mum says that about 2,000 **tourists** come here every day. Luxor is beside the River Nile. Some tourists come here by boat.

Looking back at the River Nile from the Aswan Dam

Dear Bob,

Not everything in Egypt is old! We came to see the Aswan Dam. People built it across the Nile to hold the river back. There is a big lake on the other side of the dam.

Love,

Bruce

P.S. My uncle says that the water in the dam is used to make electricity. The Aswan Dam is nearly four kilometres across, that is more than two miles.

Bedouin men making tea at their camp in the desert

Dear Lyn,

Our plane flew over a huge sandy **desert** when we crossed Egypt. We saw lots of hills in the sand. The wind blows the sand into these hills, called dunes. The desert is very dry.

Love,

Cathy

P.S. My brother says do you know about water holes called **oases**? The Bedouin people live in the desert. They travel from one oasis to another.

Bedouin girls playing backgammon

Dear Len,

I think it is too hot for sports here! The Egyptians love to play football in the winter months. Children like to play games in the afternoon, after school.

Best wishes,

John

P.S. We watched some children playing a board game called backgammon. It is a bit like draughts. They got very excited. I would like to play backgammon.

A feast at the end of Ramadan, in Cairo

Dear Carol,

Most of the **festivals** here are part of the religion of **Islam**. The month called Ramadan is a holy month. Nobody eats or drinks while it is daylight. This is called a **fast**.

Love,

Simon

P.S. Dad says that when the month is over everybody celebrates. There are big parties and people give presents. They eat a lot when the fast is over.

The Egyptian flag flying beside a
pyramid

Dear Gita,

I hope you like this picture of the Egyptian flag. It has three stripes on it. They are red, white and black. There is a golden eagle in the middle of the flag.

Love,

Diane

P.S. Dad says that the leader of Egypt is called the president. The people of Egypt choose their own leaders. This is a **democracy**. Egypt is ruled from the **capital** city, Cairo.

Glossary

Bazaar: A market where people buy and sell all kinds of things.

Capital: The town or city where people who rule the country meet. It is not always the biggest city in the country.

Delta: The place where a river breaks into many smaller rivers before it reaches the sea.

Democracy: A country where all the people choose the leaders they want to run the country.

Desert: A place where there is very little water or rain. Very few animals or plants can live there.

Fast: A time when people do not eat.

Festival: A time when people remember something special that happened in the past. Sometimes people sing and dance at a festival.

Islam: A religion. People who follow Islam are called Muslims. They believe in the teachings of Muhammad, who lived about 1,400 years ago.

Machine: Something we make which does work for us.

Oasis: A place in the desert where there is water.

Preserve: To treat something so that it keeps for a long time without going bad.

P.S.: This stands for Post Script. A postscript is the part of a card or letter which is added at the end, after the person has signed it.

Spice: Part of a plant that is dried and used to give food a stronger flavour.

Temple: A building where people go to pray.

Tourist: A person who is on holiday away from home.

Index